SMART
ESSE

THE STUDENT GUIDE TO LITERACY

IN EVERY SUBJECT

SMART LEARNING

CONTENTS

Better spelling

With a bit of care, you can spell better. Spellings can be tricky, but most words stick to rules and patterns. The strategies (ways) below can help you to improve your spelling. They are explained more fully on pages 5 to 9.

Way to spell	Explanation	Example
Sound it out	Carefully say the word out loud and make sure you write down the word, sound by tiny sound.	*Dog* has three sounds: d – o – g.
Break it down and sound it out	Break the word into syllables. Say each syllable, and write down each one.	*Target* has two syllables: tar – get.
Find the stem word	Some long words are just short words with bits stuck on.	The stem of *undo* is *do*: *un* has been stuck on the front of *do*.
Memory tricks	Invent memory games to help you remember hard words.	**R**hythm **h**elps **y**our **t**wo **h**ips **m**ove (rhythm).
Look, say, cover, write, check	Look carefully at the word, say it, cover it up, write it down, check if you are right. Repeat these steps if you have got the word wrong.	Here are examples of words that you might have to learn in this way: *eight*, *throughout*, *particle*.
Say it like it is	Some words have silent letters. When you say these words, say their silent letters too.	Wed – nes – day

Sounding it out

1 Say the word out loud slowly. Make sure you say every bit of the word properly. For example, the word *blast* starts with a *b* sound and ends with a *t* sound.

2 Now write down the word. Make sure you write letters for every sound in the word. You can hear that the word *blast* has five sounds: b – l – a – s – t.

TRY IT OUT

1 Say these words out loud and slowly: cat [3], tennis [5], remember [7]. The numbers in brackets show the number of sounds you should have found for each word.

2 Look at the list of words on page 10. Choose six of them. Say each one out loud and try to write it down without looking at the word.

WATCH OUT

There are different ways of saying some words and so you might disagree with others about how many sounds are in each word.

Breaking it down and sounding it out

This is like sounding a word out, but it is easier.

1 Take a word and break it into its parts (or syllables).

2 Say each part out loud, clearly and slowly.

3 Then try to spell each part.

For example, say *understand* slowly. You will find it has three parts: un – der – stand. If you try spelling each part and then put the parts together, you will probably manage to spell the whole word.

1   Try breaking down and sounding out these words:

   assembly   oxygen   explosion   Saturday   finally

2   Look at the words on page 10. Choose three of them. Try breaking them down and sounding them out.

Finding the stem word

A **stem word** is the main part of a word, to which bits can be added on to make other words.

Some words that sound difficult are really just ordinary words with bits added on. For example:

- *Jump* is the stem word of *jumped*. *-ed* goes on the end of lots of stem words.

- *Sudden* is the stem word of *suddenly*. *-ly* goes on the end of lots of stem words.

- *Familiar* is the stem word of *unfamiliar*. *un-* goes on the front of lots of stem words.

- *Belief* is the stem word of *disbelief*. *dis-* goes on the front of lots of stem words.

NOTE
A bit added on to a stem word is called an **affix**. An affix on the front of a stem word is called a **prefix**. An affix on the end of a stem word is called a **suffix**. *Fix* is the stem word inside *affixes*.

1 Look at the six words below. Find and write out the stem word in each one.

slowly   helpful   fearlessly
unhappy   disappear   unforgettable

2 Here are some common affixes:

in-   un-   dis-   pre-   anti-
-able   -ness   -ing   -ed   -ful

Think of a few words that have each of these affixes. Can you work out what each affix means?

Memory tricks

Some spellings can be remembered by creating silly rules for them. For example, the word *because* can be remembered by making each of its letters the start of words in a strange sentence: **B**ig **e**lephants **c**annot **a**lways **u**se **s**mall **e**xits. If you can remember the strange sentence you will also remember how to spell *elephant*. And, of course, elephants never forget.

TRY IT OUT

Try to think of an unusual way of remembering each of the words below. The hard bits are in **bold**.

choc**o**late   bisc**ui**t   defin**i**te   bus**i**ness   gover**n**ment

Look, say, cover, write, check

Many good spellers can see words in their head. They know when a word looks right or wrong. It is worth learning the *look* of words. The steps on the page 8 explain how to do this.

1 Write the word down carefully.

2 Look at it closely.

3 Say the word carefully out loud.

4 Cover it up.

5 Write it out without looking at the word.

6 Check that you have spelt it right.

If it is wrong, do it again. Start by looking closely at the word.

 Use this method to firm up your spelling of all words – even ones you have learnt to spell with other methods.

TRY IT OUT

Draw a table like the one below, but big enough to give you plenty of room.

Write the word you want to practise in the first column. Cover it up and write it again. Keep writing it until you get it right – at least once! See the example in the table.

interest	~~intrest~~	interest	

 Crossing out wrong spellings is important. It tells your eyes that the spelling is wrong.

Saying it like it is

Some words have silent letters. Try saying aloud the silent letters in a word such as *know* to remind yourself they are there. The *k* and the *w* are silent in *know*.

Here are some more examples:

- There is a silent *c* in *science*.
- We do not usually say the *o* in *chocolate*.

 You might feel silly doing this, but if your friends join in, then you can share the fun.

TRY IT OUT

In the table below, there are some words that are tricky to spell because of their silent letters. Their silent letters are shown in **bold**.

- Say each word out loud.
- Make sure you say every part of the word.

The correct spelling	Say it like this ...
We**d**nesday	Wed – nes – day
s**c**ience	sci – ence
know	k – no – w
parl**ia**ment	par – li – a – ment
choc**o**late	choc – o – late
inter**e**sting	in – ter – est – ing
bus**i**ness	bus – i – ness
ans**w**er	ans – wer

WATCH OUT

We do not all say every word in the same way. There are lots of different accents. For example, some of us *do* say the first *d* and the second *e* in *Wednesday*. There are no *right* accents, just *different* ones.

A useful spelling list

Here is a list of some words that you should definitely learn to spell before you begin your GCSE courses:

accommodate	definite	Monday	remember
although	different	muscle	safety
angle	disappear	necessary	Saturday
assembly	disappoint	parallel	secondary
autumn	effective	parliament	separate
basic	energy	pattern	straight
believe	February	persuade	surprise
biology	government	photosynthesis	through
business	height	physical	tomorrow
cause	independence	physics	Tuesday
character	independent	prepare	unnecessary
chemistry	ingredient	radiation	Wednesday
college	isosceles	ratio	weight
conclusion	knowledge	reaction	woman/women

Final tips and advice on spelling

1 If you have trouble spelling a word:
   - Use one of the six strategies on pages 5 to 9. Choose the best strategy for the word you need to spell.
   - Use the *Look, say, cover, write, check* method to firm up your spelling of all words – even ones you have learnt to spell with other methods.

2 Here are two more things you can do to find out how to spell a word:
   - Find the word in a dictionary and copy it down.
   - Ask a friend or family member.

3   Do not guess at spellings. If you use a good method, then you will spell any word better than by just guessing. If you spell a word sensibly, then anyone reading your work will know what you mean, even if you have got the spelling wrong.

4   Do not spend a long time worrying over a spelling. It is better to spell the best you can (perhaps even just concentrating on the first and last letter), and then carry on with your writing. You can always come back to the word later.

Plural

Plural means more than one. The plural of *lamp* is *lamp**s***. Words make their plural spellings in different ways.

> The four main rules for making plural spellings are:
>
> - Add -*s* to the end of the word. This is the rule for most words.
> - Add -*es* to the end of the word, e.g. *church**es**.*
> - If a word ends in a consonant + *y*, replace the -*y* with -*ies*, e.g. *bab**ies**.*
> - Add nothing at all, e.g. *fish*, or change completely, e.g. *man/men*.

NOTE Almost all the letters are **consonants**. Five letters are **vowels**: a, e, i, o, u. The letter *y* can be a consonant or a vowel. It is a consonant in *you*, but a vowel in *only*.

Adding -*s*

Most words simply add -*s* onto their end to make the plural.

Adding -es

If a word ends in a *sh, ss, ch* or *ks* sound, we add *-es* to make the plural. Here are some examples:

singular	plural	singular	plural
bush	bushes	sash	sashes
boss	bosses	kiss	kisses
church	churches	match	matches
fox	foxes	tax	taxes

Taking away -y and adding -ies

If a word ends in a consonant + *y*, then to make the plural we usually take away the *-y* and replace it with *-ies*. For example:

singular	plural	singular	plural
baby	babies	bully	bullies
lady	ladies	nappy	nappies

NOTE This way only works when the letter before the *-y* is a consonant. If a vowel comes before the *-y*, we just add *-s*. For example: *days, boys, guys, alleys*.

Adding nothing or changing completely

A few words do not add *-s* to make the plural: they stay exactly the same. Other words change completely. For example:

singular	plural	singular	plural
child	children	person	people
man	men	woman	women
fish	fish	sheep	sheep

Copy out the table below and write in the correct plurals. If you are not sure, then look carefully again at the four rules on pages 11 and 12.

singular	plural	singular	plural
hutch		ray	
car		torch	
box		cake	
family		brush	
sack		book	
bus		pulley	
tooth		mouse	

Homophone

Spelling can be tricky because:

- Some words have the same sound, but different spellings and meanings. These are called **homophones**.
- Some words have the same sound *and* the same spelling, but different meanings. These are also called homophones.

Same sound, different spellings and meanings

Here are some common homophones:

their/there	two/too/to	write/right
band/banned	I/eye	see/sea

For each of the words below, write down a homophone, e.g. *bear/bare*.

new   here   one   four   made   I'll

Same sound and spelling, different meanings

Examples of this sort of homophone include:

rose (flower / past tense of *rise*)
fit (healthy / connect neatly)
park (play area / leaving a car somewhere).

WATCH OUT

Whether a word has the same sound depends on how *you* normally say it. People in different areas say the same word in different ways. For example, in some places, these word pairs are homophones: *sales/sells*; *our/are*. Homophones are about sounds, and so are accents.

Homograph

Some words have the same spelling, but different sounds and different meanings. These are called **homographs**.

The word *row* is a homograph. Read these two sentences aloud:

The students stood in one long row.
I had a row with my sister.

The word *close* is another homograph. Read these two sentences aloud:

Please close the door.
Stay close to me.

TRY IT OUT

Below are five homographs. Use each one in two sentences as in the examples at the bottom of page 14.

wind   tear   bow   minute   number

NOTE

Homophones and homographs are both **homonyms**. The word *homonym* comes from two Greek words, which together mean 'same name'. Other common words come from Greek as well. *Homophone* means 'same sound'. *Homograph* means 'same writing'. *Telephone* means 'distant sound'. *Homosexual* means 'same sex'.

Advanced spelling rules

Here are three more sets of rules to help with your spelling:

- If a single (short) consonant follows a vowel, the vowel sound is long. If a double (long) consonant follows a vowel, the vowel sound is short.

- If the stem of a word makes sense on its own, add *-able*. If not, add *-ible*.

- Add *-tion* after most stems, especially if the stem ends in *-t* or *-e*. Add *-sion* after most stems that end in *-d*. Add *-cian* after stems that are to do with jobs.

Long–short, short–long

Normally, when a vowel is followed by a single (short) consonant, the vowel makes a long sound, e.g. *taping*. When a vowel is followed by a double (long) consonant, it makes a short sound, e.g. *tapping*.

Here are some examples of words that follow the long–short and short–long patterns:

Vowel	Long–short	Short–long
a	la<u>t</u>er, ca<u>n</u>ed	ha<u>pp</u>y, ca<u>nn</u>ed
e	Pe<u>t</u>er, me<u>t</u>er	be<u>tt</u>er
i	wri<u>ting</u>, ri<u>d</u>ing	wri<u>tt</u>en, ri<u>dd</u>en
o	ho<u>p</u>ing, <u>op</u>en	ho<u>pp</u>ing, <u>off</u>
u	tu<u>n</u>a, ta<u>p</u>ed	ru<u>nn</u>er, ta<u>pp</u>ed

WATCH OUT

Some words break the rule.

NOTE

Each of the five vowels has short and long sounds:

Vowel	Examples of short sound	Examples of long sound
a	**cap**, b**ack**, **an**, m**ad**	cape, bake, **ace**, made
e	**pet**, s**end**, **red**, n**eck**	Peter, scene, female
i	**pin**, **kit**, **him**, **give**	pine, kite, kind, lined
o	h**op**, sh**ock**, bl**ock**, c**on**	hope, **open**, cone, **only**
u	**up**, tr**ust**, m**uck**, b**utter**	Luton, cute, duty, brute

-ible or *-able*

If the stem of a word makes sense on its own, add *-able*.

If the stem of a word does not make sense on its own, add *-ible*.

The stem word of *eatable* is *eat*. The stem word of *playable* is *play*. *Eat* and *play* are whole words on their own, so they add *-able*. *Sens* is the stem of *sensible*, but there is no such word as *sens*, and that is why *sensible* is spelt with an *i*.

Here are some more *-ible* and *-able* words that stick to these rules:

washable   edible   audible   changeable

TRY IT OUT

Which ending would you add to each of these stems?

laugh-   do-   terr-   understand-   horr-   illeg-

-tion, -sion or *-cian*

These three endings sound the same, so how can you know which one to put on the end of different stems? Here are some rules:

- Add *-tion* after most stems, especially if the stem ends in *-t* or *-e* (e.g. *distract/distraction, hesitate/hesitation*).
- Add *-sion* after most stems that end in *-d* (e.g. *expand/ expansion*), or where the word only makes sense *with* the ending (e.g. *passion*).
- Add *-cian* after stems that are to do with jobs (e.g. *musician*).

There are occasional exceptions, but here are some more words that stick to the rules:

-tion	-sion	-cian
creation	comprehension	magician
ignition	mission	beautician

2: WORD CLASSES

Noun

A **noun** is a word for a person, place or thing.

Here are some examples of nouns for people and places: Sophie, Africa, Kieron, London. These nouns are names, so they start with a capital letter. These types of nouns are called **proper nouns**.

> A proper noun starts with a capital letter.

Most nouns are words for things. A thing can be something you see, hear, smell, hold, feel or imagine. For example, a table is a thing and the word *table* is a noun. However, although you cannot touch it, beauty is also a sort of thing, so the word *beauty* is also a noun. So is *thing*. So is *noun*. These types of nouns are called **common nouns**.

Most nouns are common nouns, and they usually have a **determiner** before them. Determiners put limits on nouns. Determiners include numbers and words such as: *the, a, an, this, these, some*. For example:

the tree	**some** biscuits	**this** government	**six** thoughts
that river	**an** apple	**these** doors	**one** idea

NOTE

We can divide common nouns into **countable nouns** and **non-countable nouns**. Countable nouns can be more than one, e.g. *car/cars, idea/ideas*. Non-countable nouns cannot usually be counted at all, e.g. *happiness, water*.

1 Here are some nouns of various sorts:

river	disappointment	afternoon	wall
biscuit	Leeds	Smith	happiness
tree	anger	music	government

For each noun above, decide if it is proper, countable or non-countable.

2 Write out the sentence below and underline the five nouns in it.

Without cars or buses to disturb the peace, silence settled on the street.

Adjective

Nouns often come with other words that give more information about them. Some of these words are called **adjectives**. Adjectives are sometimes called describing words.

In the six phrases below, the adjective is shown in **bold**. Each one describes the noun with it.

deep happiness
the **Labour** government
two **awful** thoughts

her **terrible** anger
a **tall** tree
this **juicy** apple

The six phrases on page 19 are examples of **noun phrases**. They are called noun phrases because the noun is the vital word in the phrase. The other words give more information about the noun. In the long noun phrases below, the noun **head word** is shown in **bold**:

> a very long and relaxing **holiday**
> this ten-year-long **reign** of terror
> those horribly cruel text **messages**

Adjectives can come after their noun as well as before it. In the examples below, the adjective is shown in **bold**:

> The flowers are **beautiful**.
> The car was **red**.
> Sarah is **tall**.

WATCH OUT

1   Using lots of adjectives or long noun phrases can make your writing worse. It is often better to choose just one right word, rather than using lots, e.g. *catastrophe* might be better than *huge problem*.

2   Many words can be adjectives *or* nouns. It depends on what they *do*.

TRY IT OUT

Look at these two sentences:

> I like music.
> I went into the music shop.

In one sentence the word *music* is a noun (a thing). In the other, *music* is an adjective (which gives more information about a thing). Which of the sentences is which?

Pronoun

A **pronoun** is a word used in place of a noun.

Here are the most common pronouns:

I	you	she	he	it	we	they	this
me	you	her	him	it	us	them	that
my	your	her	his	its	our	their	these
mine	yours	hers	his	its	ours	theirs	those

We use pronouns to avoid repeating the same noun. Look at how clumsy this piece of writing is:

> Jamie sat on the table. The table was too weak for Jamie. The table collapsed. Jamie fell on the floor.

The writing is clumsy mainly because *Jamie* and *table* keep getting repeated. Here are the sentences rewritten and improved with pronouns and connectives (for more about connectives, see pages 25 to 27):

> Jamie sat on the table, but because **it** was too weak for **him**, **it** collapsed and **he** fell on the floor.

WATCH OUT

Only use pronouns if you are sure that your reader will understand them. Weak writers use lots of confusing pronouns. Here is some writing that is bad because we do not always know who "she" refers to. Is it Laila or her mother?

> Laila saw her mother outside the supermarket. This was not surprising as she was often there. In fact she worked there. She walked in and picked up a basket, but she did not see her.

Verb

A **verb** is the most important type of word. Nothing makes sense without a verb. Verbs are being, having and doing words. Here are three sentences with the verbs shown in **bold**:

- I **am** a student. (*Am* is part of *to be*, a being verb.)
- I **have** geography next lesson. (*Have* is obviously a having verb, but *had* is also a having verb, and so is *has*.)
- I **sing**. (*Sing* is a doing verb: *What do you do? I sing.*)

Here are some other doing verbs:

sit	think	eat	take
enjoy	compare	evaluate	do

Changes according to tense

Verbs are tricky because they change according to **tense** (past or present). To show that the action (the verb) has happened in the past, we often just add -*ed* to the end of the verb. However, many common verbs change in odd ways to show the past tense. Look at the examples below:

Present tense	Past tense
I enjoy	I enjoy**ed**
She loves	She lov**ed**
They evaluate	They evaluat**ed**
You run	You r**a**n
I swim	I sw**a**m
We think	We th**ought**

Changes according to who is doing the action

Verbs also change their endings according to who is doing them. For example, see below how three common verbs change their endings in the present tense:

	to be	to have	to see
I	am	have	see
You	are	have	see
She, he or it	is	has	sees
We	are	have	see
You	are	have	see
They	are	have	see

The headings in the table give the **infinitive** form of each verb. The infinitive is the basic verb with *to* in front of it.

Auxiliary verb

Auxiliary verbs are used with other verbs to show tenses in subtle ways, including the future tense.

That is one reason why *have* and *be* are such common verbs. They are often used as auxiliary verbs. Look at how *to have* and *to be* can be used in this way:

Have	Be
I **have** met him.	I **am** singing.
I **had** met him.	I **was** singing.
I will **have** met him.	I have **been** singing.
I **have had** to meet him.	I will **be** singing.
I **had had** to meet him.	I will have **been** singing.

Sometimes verbs are grouped together in a verb chain (**verb phrase**) to show a particular tense. The sentence below has three auxiliary verbs leading up to the verb *singing*.

I **will have been** singing all day on Thursday.

WATCH OUT

We all speak in our own way. However, writing is not just our voices written down. Most writing has to be in **Standard English**. This is formal English: the English we use with strangers, not friends. This means, for example, that we should write *we were*, not *we was*, and *I did*, not *I done*.

TRY IT OUT

There are twelve verbs in this short piece of writing.

> He laid back and shut his eyes. Soon he was thinking of that morning and the drive to Susie's house. Breathing deeply, he remembered every inch of the journey that he had took through the familiar city streets. He could clearly picture in his imagination when and where it had suddenly all gone wrong.

1 Find all twelve verbs.
2 Which two verbs are *not* written in correct Standard English?
3 How should they have been written in Standard English?

WATCH OUT

Some words can be used as a verb *or* as a noun. The word *drive* is usually a verb, but in the writing above, it is a noun. The word *picture* is usually a noun, but here it is used as a verb.

Here are three words: walk, move, flower.

Write two sentences for each word. In one sentence, use the word as a noun. In the other sentence, use the word as a verb.

Here is an example, using the word *climb*:

> We will **climb** the mountain. (verb)
> The mountain was a hard **climb**. (noun)

Connective

Connectives are the words and phrases we use to connect ideas when we speak or write. The table on page 26 groups connectives by what they are good for.

NOTE

Connective is a broad term that includes:

- conjunctions (e.g. *and*, *because*)
- relative pronouns (e.g. *who*, *which*)
- adverbials (e.g. *however*, *therefore*).

Using connectives to join ideas and thoughts

Connectives join up ideas and thoughts. Look at these two sentences:

> Duke William won the Battle of Hastings. He had a well-trained and well-led army.

We can only guess that there is a connection between the two statements. However, we could probably join the two sentences with the connective *because*:

> Duke William won the Battle of Hastings **because** he had a well-trained and well-led army.

Connectives also let you change the order of the statements to change the emphasis. For example:

Because he had a well-trained and well-led army, Duke William won the Battle of Hastings.

Connectives and their uses

Adding	Exceptions	Cause and effect
and	However	because
also	although / even though	so
as well as	unless	for
in addition	except	Therefore
Furthermore	if / even if	Thus
Time	**Putting in order**	**Contrasting**
when	next	whereas
whenever	then	instead of
while	firstly/secondly/thirdly	alternatively
Meanwhile	finally	but
since	after/Afterwards	on the other hand
until		yet
Giving examples	**Emphasising**	**Comparing**
for example	above all	Equally
such as	in particular	In the same way
for instance	particularly	Similarly
	especially	

NOTE Connectives in the table that start with a capital letter are usually only used at the *start* of a sentence, *not* in the middle.

TRY IT OUT

Here are three pairs of sentences:

> We put on our safety goggles. We were using the sander.
> We added some universal indicator to the liquid. It turned red.
> I went to see my teacher. I did not like him.

Now practise using connectives to join the sentences together.

1 Join each pair of sentences to make one sentence, using a suitable connective from the table on page 26.
2 Do it again, by choosing different connectives.
3 Try *starting* your new sentences with connectives.
4 Try writing some of your own sentences, using connectives that you have not used so far.

Adverb

Adverbs give more information

- about verbs
- about adjectives
- about other adverbs.

Adverbs about verbs

These adverbs give *how, when* or *where* information about verbs.

In the examples below, the adverb tells us *how* something was done. The adverbs are shown in **bold**.

> He ran **quickly**.
> She sang **beautifully**.

Adverbs also give information about *where* or *when* something was done. For example:

They played **here**. (where)
They played **yesterday**. (when)

Adverbs can be longer than a single word. Sometimes a whole phrase can do the work of an adverb. These phrases are often called **adverbials**. Sometimes they are called **adverb phrases**. Here are some examples with the adverbials shown in **bold**:

They played **near the fence**. (where)
They sang **on Tuesday evenings**. (when)
She ran **with a clumsy style**. (how)

WATCH OUT

Adverbs often end in *-ly*, but not always. In the sentence you have just read, the words *often* and *always* are both adverbs because they give more information about the verb *end*.

TRY IT OUT

Copy out the four sentences below and underline the adverb or adverbial in each sentence.

She played happily.
I will see you tomorrow.
I found it under the table.
Last week I lost my tennis racket.

Adverbs about adjectives

Adverbs also give more information about adjectives. Look at this sentence:

> She drove a **bright** red car.

The word *bright* gives more information about the adjective *red*. *Bright* belongs with *red,* not *car,* so in this sentence the word *bright* is an adverb.

TRY IT OUT

In the four sentences below, *one* of the words in bold is *not* an adverb: it is an adjective.

> It was a **long**, gloomy tunnel.
> He was **deeply** unhappy.
> She was wearing a **dark** blue coat.
> The car was **very** dirty.

1 Which word in **bold** is an adjective?
2 How do you know?

Adverbs about other adverbs

Sometimes we use adverbs and adverbials to give more information about another adverb.

In each example below, the word in **bold** gives more information about the underlined adverb:

> He ran **very** <u>fast</u>. (*very* and *fast* are both adverbs.)
> He walked **quite** <u>slowly</u>. (*quite* and *slowly* are both adverbs.)

Full stop (.)

A full stop marks the end of a sentence. The next sentence starts with a capital letter.

Comma (,)

Many good writers disagree over when to use a comma. Even your teachers might not agree about when to use a comma. Commas have two main and very important jobs:

- to make things clearer for your reader
- to separate things in a list.

Commas to make things clear

A comma makes the reader pause, and that pause often helps them to understand what you *meant* to say. Read this sentence:

> Arjun chose pizza and chips and lasagne was what
> Sarah chose.

By the time you read the word *was*, you might already think that Arjun chose pizza, chips *and* lasagne. This confuses you because you suddenly discover that lasagne was what Sarah chose. (She might even have chosen *chips* and lasagne.) A comma after *chips* would have stopped the confusion:

> Arjun chose pizza and chips, and lasagne was what
> Sarah chose.

Here are two sentences that need commas:

> Although we kept stirring the sauce it still went a bit lumpy and we had to blend it smooth. If we could do it again we would pour the milk in more slowly and we would stir it more carefully.

Write out the two sentences above and put in commas where you think they would help to make the meaning clear.

Commas in lists

Sometimes we use commas to avoid repeating *and*.

Here is a sentence that keeps using *and*:

> For my birthday I got some chocolates **and** some money **and** a new phone **and** a tent **and** three books.

The sentence sounds clumsy. It could have been written like this, with commas and only one *and*:

> For my birthday I got some chocolates **,** some money **,** a new phone **,** a tent **and** three books.

Sometimes we use a short list of words to describe something:

> I bought a shiny **,** fast car.
> I had a huge **,** juicy **,** expensive burger.

Here, commas have been used instead of the word *and*.

WATCH OUT

You can only put a comma into a list where you could use the word *and* instead of a comma. For example, this is wrong:

> The substance had become very **,** smelly, dark and thick.

You cannot put *and* after *very*, so the comma there is wrong.

Which comma should *not* be in each sentence below?

> The foods I like best are chocolate, pasta, spicy, chicken and chips.

> To improve my sauce I could have added butter, English, mustard and cream.

Speech marks ("...")

You should use speech marks:

- to show what someone says in a story or a report
- to show a **quotation** (words that someone else said or wrote).

NOTE To show speech or quotations you can use double ("...") or single ('...') speech marks, but stick to one or the other: *do not* use one, then the other.

Showing what someone says

Use speech marks to show the actual words (**direct speech**) that someone says. Speech marks are most often used in stories when you are writing **dialogue** (the speech between two or more characters).

Here is an example of dialogue in a story:

> "I'm going home through the cemetery. It's quicker," said Danielle, challenging Harry.
> "Well, you'll be going on your own then," Harry replied.

The speech marks show the reader which words have been said by a character in the story. The words that are *not* inside the speech marks are what the storyteller (**narrator**) is telling us.

There are three rules for showing direct speech:

- Put speech marks ("...") at the start and at the end of the words that a character says.
- You must put the right punctuation mark for the speech – comma (,), full stop (.), question mark (?) or exclamation mark(!) – inside the end speech mark (").
- Start a new paragraph every time you change the speaker. (You can see this in the dialogue on page 32.)

TRY IT OUT

The three rules are obeyed in the dialogue below. Copy out the dialogue and label it to show where each rule is used.

> "Ooh, are you scared?" Danielle laughed. She couldn't believe it.
>
> "Of course," said Harry. "Not!" He ran screaming through the cemetery gates.
>
> "Wait!" Danielle yelled as she raced after Harry, giggling helplessly.

Showing quotations

Sometimes we want to use someone else's words in our own writing: we want to tell our reader what someone else has said or written. When we do this we are quoting them: we are using a quotation.

For example, if you were writing about the cemetery gates story above, you might write:

> We know that Danielle is not scared because when she chases Harry she is "giggling helplessly".

The speech marks around "giggling helplessly" show that they are not your words: they are a quotation from someone else's writing.

Punctuation to end sentences

There are three punctuation marks to end a sentence:

- a full stop
- an exclamation mark
- a question mark.

(See pages 43 to 53 to find out more about writing sentences.)

Full stop (.)

This is the most common way of ending a sentence. (See page 30.)

Exclamation mark (!)

An exclamation mark is used at the end of a sentence which is a command or a shout. For example:

> I'm over here, Krishnan!
> Just tell me what you want!

Exclamation marks are mainly used in speech. Sometimes –
as in the sentence below – an exclamation mark expresses
surprise or even shock:

> When he looked in the fridge, he found that everything had
> been eaten!

Question mark (?)

You must put a question mark at the end of a question.
For example:

> Have you ever tasted a freshly-made, crumbly cheesecake?
> How was the costume appropriate to the dance idea?
> What techniques does the artist use?

TRY IT OUT

Copy out the five sentences below and finish each one with
an exclamation mark, a question mark or a full stop. Use the
punctuation that best fits the end of the sentence.

> What happened when the light ray was shone into the mirror
> Mobile phones will be confiscated
> The jewels had simply disappeared
> The vacuum former had broken down
> Who knows how much longer we will have to suffer this chaos

More advanced punctuation

Apostrophe (')

An **apostrophe** has two uses:

- to show who owns something (e.g. *John's bike*)
- to show where letters have been missed out (e.g. *you're*).

The two uses of an apostrophe are not hard to understand, but many people get into a muddle when they use them.

Showing belonging/ownership

The apostrophe + s is a neat and easy way to show who or what owns something.

> To show ownership, we put the apostrophe + s straight after the owner. For example:
>
> If Ollie owns a bike, it is Ollie**'s** bike.

It would be natural to say, "I rode Ollie's bike." It would be very unnatural to say, "I rode the bike that belongs to Ollie."

The 'owner' does not have to be a person. For example:

The flower's petals were red.
The river's banks were being eroded.

The owner in the first sentence is *the flower*. The owner in the second sentence is *the river*. In each sentence the apostrophe is placed straight after the owner.

1 If a name already ends with an *s* (e.g. *James*, *Jones*), then you can just add an apostrophe instead of apostrophe + *s* (e.g. *James'*).

2 The owner can be more than one person or thing. In the two sentences below, the apostrophes are also placed straight after the owners:

>   **The flowers'** petals were red.
>   **The rivers'** banks were being eroded.

In the first sentence we are now talking about the petals of *more than one* flower. We know this because the apostrophe comes after *flowers*, not *flower*. In the second sentence, it is the banks of more than one river that are being eroded.

Showing where letters are left out

Below are three sentences that have apostophes in place of some letters. The full words are shown at the end of each sentence.

>   She **wouldn't** play with us. (would not)
>   That **doesn't** make sense! (does not)
>   **Wasn't** it any use to you? (was it not)

Replacing missed out letters with an apostrophe is simple. Even when two or more letters are missed out together, you just use one apostrophe, e.g. *cannot* becomes *can't*.

Leaving letters out is often called **omission** or **contraction**.

WATCH OUT

In formal writing, do not use apostrophes to miss out letters. Use the full word instead. For example, use *are not* instead of *aren't*.

TRY IT OUT

Write out the following phrases, changing them into their shortened form with an apostrophe. One has been done for you as an example:

do not (don't)
should not
you are
will not

The last one is a bit of a cheat. It does not stick exactly to the rule.

WATCH OUT

The words *its* and *it's* mean different things. Logically both deserve an apostrophe, but they don't both get one.

its means 'of it' as in *I picked the kettle up by **its** handle.* Here the kettle 'owns' the handle.

it's means 'it is' as in ***It's** a lovely day.* Here the letter *i* has been missed out of 'it is'.

We only use an apostrophe in *it's* when we miss out a letter (*contraction*). For example:

It's wonderful that **its** handle is covered in plastic insulation.

Colon (:)

The colon has two main uses:

- to introduce a list (or sometimes an idea, an example or a quotation)

- to mean *that is to say* or *and that is / those are*.

Introducing a list

Sometimes a colon is used to introduce a list. Here are some examples:

> For Christmas I got the following: books, money, clothes and a new phone.

> Italian chefs insist that to make a great bolognese sauce you need these ingredients: olive oil; streaky pancetta bacon; chopped onions; crushed garlic; diced carrots; a stick of celery; lean minced beef; red wine; chopped tomatoes; bay leaves.

To mean that is to say ... *or* and that is ...

Sometimes a colon is used instead of phrases like *that is to say* or *and that is*. For example:

> There is one thing I hate about buses: they are unreliable. (the colon replaces *and that is*)

> I have just two words for you: go away. (the colon replaces *and they are*)

Semi-colon (;)

The semi-colon has two main uses:

- to hint that one statement explains another
- to separate multi-word items in a list.

Hinting that one statement explains another

Here are two statements that may or may not be linked:

Amelia was searching for her bag. Solomon was smirking.

If we separate the two statements with a semi-colon instead of a full stop, then we are hinting that one action is caused by the other. Solomon is smirking *because* he knows where the bag is; he has probably hidden it.

TRY IT OUT

Explain what each of these sentences suggests:

My heart is racing; I have been training.
I revised thoroughly; I did well in my exam.

Separating multi-word items in a list

We can use semi-colons to make a complicated list, where each item is more than one word, clearer. For example:

I needed an apple; three fresh, firm celery stalks; a cup of cooked, drained rice; and a chopped onion.

(See page 39 for another example of how to use semi-colons in a list.)

Dashes, brackets, parenthetic commas

All three of these types of punctuation are used to surround a piece of information that is not essential. Brackets and dashes have almost the same use. Whether a writer uses one or the other is often just a matter of what they prefer.

Dashes

Dashes separate information that is not vital from the rest of a sentence. For example:

> Flow – **a key dynamic in dance** – is about how lightly or strongly you perform a sequence.

The dashes provide information that you might want to ignore for the time being. For example, some readers of this sentence might not need to be reminded of the information inside the dashes.

A single dash can be used at the end of a sentence: see an example of this in the next sentence about brackets.

Brackets

Brackets also separate information that is not vital from the rest of the sentence – like the dashes in the dance example above. However, brackets can also be used for a comment (an aside) from the writer to the reader. For example:

> Some people think this is wrong **(and only last week someone complained to me about this)**, but I disagree.

Brackets can also be used round a whole sentence. Again, the information in the sentence would be an aside or not essential. If you use brackets in this way, then the sentence inside the paragraph must be fully punctuated. For example:

> I was trying to use the typical techniques of a particular artist, Maryanne Jacobsen. (Jacobsen is a contemporary artist, who began painting in 2006.)

Parenthetic commas

Pairs of commas can also be used rather like dashes and brackets. However, commas used in this way (**in parenthesis**) are normally used to repeat the same information in a different way. For example:

Narinder Kaur**, the shop manager,** soon arrived. (Narinder Kaur *is* the shop manager.)

The government's demographers, **Leo and Ella Jones,** use pyramid models to show the structure of the population. (Leo and Ella Jones *are* the government's demographers.)

TRY IT OUT

Each of the sentences below should use brackets, dashes or parenthetic commas. Write them out, putting in the most appropriate punctuation. A forward slash (/) shows where your punctuation should go.

The PH indicator / the litmus / was dipped in the cola.

Storms can be very powerful / and recently they have done a lot of damage /.

Some European countries / for example, Spain, Switzerland and Sweden / wanted to stay out of the Second World War.

NOTE

Another useful piece of punctuation is the **ellipsis** (…). We use these three dots to show where words have been left out. An ellipsis is particularly useful when you want to leave out an irrelevant part of a quotation. For example:

When Macbeth hears that his wife is dead he says that "Life's … a tale told by an idiot …".

The ellipsis shows your reader that you have chosen only the part of the quotation that is relevant to the point you are making.

Writing better sentences

A **sentence** is a complete thought, statement or question.

A sentence must make sense, start with a capital letter and
have a full stop (.) – or a question mark or exclamation mark –
to show where it ends.

There are four simple rules for good sentences:

- Put a capital letter at the beginning and a full stop
  (or question mark / exclamation mark) at the end.
- Start them in different ways.
- Do not make them too long.
- Do not make them all the same length.

Read the sentences below. Notice how each sentence is about
a different part of the whole topic: the Roman invasion.

> Nearly two thousand years ago, the Romans
> invaded Britain. They landed their soldiers on the
> south coast. Pushing north and west, they gradually
> overcame the British tribes that fought against them.

The first sentence is long but not too long. It starts with time
("Nearly two thousand years ago …") and makes us wait for the
real information, which is about the invasion.

The third sentence ("Pushing north and west …") has its
main information – that the Romans beat the British tribes –
in the middle. It starts with something that sounds interesting.

So, these sentences:

- are different lengths
- are arranged differently (have different structures).

Essentially that is what teachers mean when they ask you to vary your sentences: make them different lengths and arrange them in different ways.

Varying sentence structure

To vary the structure of your sentences, you can start them with something that is not the main point. For example:

> You will be able to take unwanted cookers and fridges to the new recycling centre when it has been built.

It is not a bad sentence, but you could change the structure:

> When it has been built, you will be able to take unwanted cookers and fridges to the new recycling centre.

> The new recycling centre – when it has been built – will be the place where you can take unwanted cookers and fridges.

TRY IT OUT

Below is a student's report on a zoo visit. The sentences need more variety and better organisation.

Rewrite the report so that it uses good sentences that *stick to* the four rules on page 43. Do not change the information, but *do* change the way some or all of the sentences have been written.

We went to the zoo. We had fun. We learnt some useful facts. We learnt about what animals eat. We also learnt about animals that are in danger of becoming extinct because people are ruining their habitats and other animals that are dying out because greedy people are killing them for their fur or for their tusks or other things that they have got that people want.

Making sentences start better

To make your sentences better, trying beginning them with:

- *-ing* words (e.g. *Running* …, *Lifting* …, *Hoping* …)
- *-ed* words (e.g. *Exhausted*, …; *Embarrassed*, …)
- words that show time (e.g. *Last week*, …; *During the next lesson*, …)
- words that show place (e.g. *Deep in the woods*, …; *Under the table*, …)

Here are some more examples:

- Pour**ing** the acid into the test tube, we took care not to spill any.
- Peer**ing** into the darkened rodent tanks, I saw a rat.
- Asham**ed** of what I had done, I felt I had to say sorry.
- Astonish**ed** by the size of the spiders, I jumped backwards.
- **At ten past two this afternoon**, the coach will return to school. (time)
- **In the summer of 1914**, the First World War began. (time)
- **At the bottom of the test tube**, the liquid began to darken. (place)
- **In the Sahara Desert**, there is very little rainfall. (place)
- Liv**ing in Germany in the late 1930s**, Jews were terrified about what might happen to them. (*-ing*, place, time)

TRY IT OUT

Here are some sentence starters. Write them out and then finish the sentences in ways that make sense.

Trying not to splash the spaghetti sauce, …
Embarrassed, …
Just down the road from my house, …
That morning …

WATCH OUT

Do not overdo it. Change the order of your sentences to make them clearer and more interesting, not just for the sake of it.

Simple, compound and complex sentences

A sentence must have a verb (see pages 22 to 25). For example:

She was happy and lively.

This is a complete sentence because it has a verb (*was*). Now consider this:

Happy and lively.

This is not a sentence because it is incomplete; it has no verb.

Simple sentences

A **simple sentence** is one that has only one verb (or one verb chain).

Here is an example of a very short, simple sentence:

I shouted.

It has one verb – *shouted* – and is complete.

TRY IT OUT

Below are four more simple sentences. Copy out the sentences and underline the verb or verb chain in each sentence. The first has been done for you.

She <u>lost</u> her bag in the hall.

They had been hiding round the corner.

The litmus paper was dipped in the solution.

John's dance performance for the exam was absolutely stunning.

WATCH OUT

Simple sentences only have one verb but they are not always short sentences. Look at this one:

Most Kenyans **depend** on agriculture for food and income.

The only verb in that sentence is *depend*.

This simple sentence is even longer:

However, two-thirds of the Kenyan land mass **is** semi-arid to arid, with low and unreliable rainfall.

There is only one verb in this long sentence: *is*.

Compound sentences

A **compound sentence** is two simple sentences joined together with a conjunction.

> **NOTE**
>
> A **conjunction** is a type of connective. Conjunctions join parts of a sentence together. Conjunctions introduce clauses. Common conjunctions include *and*, *but*, *or, because*, *when*, *although*.

Here are three examples of compound sentences:

> We dipped the litmus paper in the solution, and it turned blue.
> Kenya depends on agriculture, but rainfall in Kenya is low.
> You can buy shortcrust pastry, or you can make your own.

Compound sentences are useful for adding new thoughts as they occur to you.

WATCH OUT

Make sure you do not write very long compound sentences by using *and* and *then* over and over again. Also, try not to use *and then*.

Complex sentences

All **complex sentences** have one main clause and at least one subordinate clause.

A **main clause**:

- roughly makes sense on its own
- is the main point of the sentence
- is not introduced by a conjunction.

A **subordinate clause**:

- gives more information about the main clause
- is usually introduced by a connective (see pages 25 to 27).

NOTE

Some people call a subordinate clause a **dependent clause** because it cannot stand on its own: it *depends* on the main clause, so it is dependent.

TRY IT OUT

Here is a complex sentence with three clauses:

> Even though I could have sanded it down more smoothly, I am pleased with my bookend because it is my best work so far in design and technology.

1 Copy out the sentence.
2 Underline the main clause in one colour.
3 Underline the two subordinate clauses in a different colour.

Varying the order of clauses in a sentence

In each complex sentence below, the conjunction is marked in **bold** and the subordinate clause is <u>underlined</u>. Note that the main clause does not have to come first.

> **When** <u>we dipped it in the solution</u>, the litmus paper turned blue.

> **Although** <u>rainfall in the country is low</u>, Kenya depends on agriculture.

> You can buy shortcrust pastry **if** <u>you do not want to make your own</u>.

1 Look at the table below. Choose one sentence from the left-hand column and one from the right-hand column.

2 Then try to connect them using a conjunction from the middle column.

3 Do the same with other pairs. Try all sorts of combinations. Try putting the conjunction at the beginning sometimes. For example:

Because it rang, she looked at her phone.

we laughed	because	he cried
the girl stood up	although	her back was aching
he was unhappy	when	it rang
she looked at her phone	unless	the teacher frowned
they jumped	whereas	the roof leaked

Other ways to start sentences

Sometimes subordinate clauses are introduced, not by a conjunction but by a **non-finite verb**. A non-finite verb is one that does not have a subject: for example, *running*, not *I run*. *I* is the subject of *run*. (For more on subjects, see the section on *active* and *passive* on pages 52 and 53.)

Below are some examples of complex sentences with subordinate clauses that start with non-finite verbs. The subordinate clause is underlined and the non-finite verb is in **bold**.

To thicken the sauce, you will need to use some flour.
Laughing hysterically, Keisha bounced on the trampoline.
Ashamed of what he had done, Declan apologised.

Designing sentences for effect

Long sentences are not always better than short ones. Complex sentences are not better than simple ones. What makes sentences better is *variety*, and designing them for the desired *effect*. Always design your sentences for the effect you want.

Look at how one student has tried to use sentence variety to create suspense:

> Leaning on the garden wall, Jim sensed that he was being watched. The wind sighed through the abandoned house. Its grimy, cracked windows stared blankly. The full moon slipped from behind the dirty clouds, and the sudden glow of moonlight spread a ghastly sheet of light across the street. Jim shivered. Hardly daring to turn his head, he peered over his shoulder at the house, dreading what he might see – or what might see him.

Notice how the student uses shorter and simple sentences when he wants the reader to slow down and feel worried. The very short sentence, "Jim shivered.", almost makes the reader hold their breath. Longer sentences are often used for more detailed, atmospheric description.

Active and passive

Sentences can be written in two different voices – the **active voice** or the **passive voice**. Here is the same sentence written in the two different ways:

Felix cooked lunch. (active)
Lunch was cooked by Felix. (passive)

In both sentences the verb is *cooked*. Normally the doer (the **subject**) of the verb is placed before the verb and the thing or person that is 'done to' (the **object**) is placed after. That is how the first sentence is arranged: it is in the active voice. The second version of the sentence swaps *Felix* and *lunch* so that the doer, *Felix*, comes after the verb. The second sentence is in the passive voice.

Here are two more pairs of examples:

Blood carries food and oxygen. (active)
Food and oxygen are carried by blood. (passive)

Jess lost the keys. (active)
The keys had been lost by Jess. (passive)

Although the active and passive versions of the sentences have the same information, they draw our attention to different things. More importantly, though, the passive allows the doer to be completely removed from the sentence. Look at this passive sentence:

The keys had been lost.

This passive sentence gives the important information – the loss of the keys – but it protects Jess from blame.

Imagine this scene at school: a boy rushes up to a teacher on break duty and blurts out, "Come quickly. One of the hall windows has been smashed."

The boy did *not* say, "Come quickly. Lee has smashed one of the hall windows." The boy could be protecting Lee, but he could also simply be concentrating on what really matters right now: what happened, not who did it.

TRY IT OUT

1   Rewrite the active sentence below in the passive.
    Start your passive sentence with: *When the litmus paper was dipped ...*

    When we dipped the litmus paper in the solution it turned blue.

2   Here are two more active sentences:

    The cable carries the electricity.
    Riya hid John's bag.

    a   Rewrite these sentences as passives.
    b   See if you can hide the doer (*Riya*) in the second sentence.

Two common text types

Newspaper report

Here is an example of the sort of report you might find in a newspaper:

Headline   First line

Devon buzzard is a real-life angry bird

Over the last month an angry buzzard has launched several vicious attacks on cyclists in Devon.

One rider was struck on the back of the head as she was cycling on a main road near Holsworthy yesterday. There have been at least four similar attacks in recent weeks.

Joan Higgins, from the Feathered Friends Society, said, "Buzzards normally stay well away from humans, but perhaps this one is protecting a nearby nest."

The latest victim, Alex Legowska, secretary of the Devon branch of the National Cycling Club, reported: "It was shocking. There was no warning. I felt a sharp blow, a scratch on my face and a very big fright!"

Cyclists are worrying about how dangerous these attacks might become. "Someone is going to lose their balance and fall into oncoming traffic," warned another member of the NCC.

A cycling time-trial scheduled to take place on the route of the attacks has been postponed for the time being. It is unclear why the buzzard has a grudge against cyclists in particular.

Main story

Typical features of a newspaper report

The **headline** is:

- in large, bold type
- worded in a catchy way. (Here there is a jokey reference to the game *Angry Birds*.)

The first line is also in bold type, which is slightly larger than the main story. This line provides basic information on:

- what (buzzard attacks)
- when (over the last month)
- where (in Devon)
- who (a buzzard/cyclists).

The main story:

- provides more detail to support the first sentence or paragraph
- is less dramatic than the headline and first line
- includes witness statements/quotations
- suggests what might happen next and what people are worried about.
- is *sometimes* set out in columns (as on page 54).

Formal letter

A formal letter should be set out as in the example on page 56.

WATCH OUT

These days people often write emails rather than letters. However, a formal email should be written in a formal way. It should be properly spelt and punctuated; the grammar should be correct; and it should be laid out neatly.

The National Cycling Club (Devon)
PO Box 39
Holsworthy
Devon
EX22 8PJ

The letter writer's address (not their name) goes at the top.

Ms Joan Higgins
Feathered Friends Society
Nuttall
Devon
PM32 8YB

The name and address of the person being written to goes here.

14 January 2014

The date the letter is written.

Dear Ms Higgins

Always start with Dear … .

I know that you will always defend buzzards and every other bird, and I do not want you to think that I am anti-bird in any way. However, we cyclists are suffering a tricky and potentially dangerous problem …

[This could be a long letter and might go on to a second page.]

Yours sincerely

Use Yours faithfully if you started with Dear sir or madam.

Alex Legowska

The writer signs their name here.

Alex Legowska
Secretary

The name (and position) of the writer.

Paragraphs

A **paragraph** is one chunk of writing, usually on one topic, within a whole text.

There are two ways to start a new paragraph:

- Miss out a line.
- Start in from the margin.

Missing out a line

Look at how the paragraphs in this student's letter are positioned:

I am writing to you to support the building of a new sports centre. I think that a sports centre would be more use to the public than a new school, because we already have three schools in our town, and I believe that building a sports centre would be more practical for our community.

Firstly, if we had a sports centre in our town it would give more people the opportunity to get involved in sports and for them to stay fit and healthy. Another practical benefit is it would give the teenagers of our community a chance to do something and enjoy themselves, which we would hope would stop them getting into trouble and keep them off the streets. There would be various activities available for all ages, such as swimming, yoga, football, boxing, dance and many more.

Secondly, everyone will be able to use a sports centre. Everyone under the age of 18 can go for free and everyone over the age of 18 will only have to pay a small fee of £18 per month, which will give them access to the gym whenever and for as long as they wish.

So, in conclusion ...

Starting in from the margin

In contrast, each paragraph in this version starts in from the margin (is indented):

> I am writing to you to support the building of a new sports centre. I think that a sports centre would be more use to the public than a new school, because we already have three schools in our town, and I believe that building a sports centre would be more practical for our community.
>
> Firstly, if we had a sports centre in our town it would give more people the opportunity to get involved in sports and for them to stay fit and healthy. It would also give the teenagers of our ...

WATCH OUT

Use *only one* of these two ways of starting a new paragraph in each piece of writing. Do not use both ways.

When should you start a new paragraph?

Use paragraphs to help your reader to follow your ideas. Start a new paragraph when you change what you are writing about.

In a story or report, start a new paragraph to change the time or place. For example:

Later that day ...
Meanwhile, over at Luke's house ...

How to start a new paragraph

A piece of writing can be hard to follow if the writer keeps changing topic without warning. Try to stick to these rules:

- Start each paragraph with a clear and simple point that lets your reader know what that paragraph is going to be about. Some people call this the **topic sentence**: it gives the topic of the paragraph.

- Try to link each paragraph to what you have already written so that the reader can feel that this is a new topic that *fits into* the whole piece of writing.

Linking paragraphs

Look again at the writing about the sports centre on page 57. This is how it is organised:

Paragraph 1 Explaining the student's purpose and belief
Paragraph 2 Point 1: opportunities to get fit and healthy
Paragraph 3 Point 2: cost
Paragraph 4 Conclusion

The student has used a very simple way of linking: he just says "Firstly", "Secondly" and "in conclusion". However, there are lots of ways to link paragraphs and help your reader to understand where you are going with your ideas.

Below are two other ways the student could have started paragraph 2 to link it back to paragraph 1. The words that link back to paragraph 1 are shown in **bold**.

One practical benefit would be that it would help the **community** to stay fit and healthy.

A **new school** would be **useful**, but what could be more useful than the chance to stay fit and healthy?

TRY IT OUT

1 Look again at paragraph 3 on page 57. Write a better version of the first sentence:

Secondly, everyone will be able to use a sports centre.

   a Use a link that is more helpful than the word "Secondly".

   b Use at least one of these words in your sentence: activities, cost, practical.

2 Try making your sentence into a question.

Using PEE to organise and develop paragraphs

PEE stands for point, example, explanation. This is how PEE works:

● Make a clear and relevant **point**.

● Give an **example** of that point. (The example could be a quotation or another form of evidence.)

● **Explain** how your example supports your point.

The paragraph on page 61 is from an English exam answer on a section of the novel, *Of Mice and Men*. The exam question was:

Explore how the language in this part of the novel influences your view of Lennie and Curley.

This is the start of the student's answer. See how she uses PEE to guide her response.

The first two sentences make a clear overall **point**: Curley is a bully, Lennie is the victim.

The reader gets the idea that although Curley is tiny, he is to blame for the fight, and he is a bully. Lennie is the innocent victim. Curley's aggression is shown in two main uses of language. Firstly, Steinbeck shows Curley's aggression through his use of emotive language. **We are told that Curley's "rage exploded".** "Rage" is a stronger word than anger and emphasises how angry Curley is. "Exploded" further emphasises the strength of his feelings and suggests that he has lost all self-control. Secondly, Steinbeck also shows Curley's aggression through his use of swear words to insult Lennie. Curley calls him a "big bastard"; a "son-of-bitch" and a "dirty little rat". The swearing and insults make us even less sympathetic to Curley.

Point: "Curley's aggression ..." introduces the first sub-point.

Example of emotive language.

Explains the **effect**.

TRY IT OUT

1 Read the notes to see how the student uses PEE after "Firstly".

2 Add your own notes to show how the student uses PEE after "Secondly".

(See pages 68 to 70 for more advice on using PEE.)

Essays and longer pieces of writing

A few minutes spent on planning your writing is time well spent – even during an exam. This section will take you through the example of planning a response to the following essay question (or task):

> *Has modern technology improved our lives?*
> *Write about at least three examples of modern*
> *technology, and explore the effects they have*
> *had on people's lives.*

The following steps are a useful way to plan a good piece of writing:

1 Make sure you understand the question and what you must do.
2 Jot down ideas for the content of your answer.
3 Organise those thoughts into groups. These will become paragraphs.
4 Decide on a topic for each paragraph.
5 Sequence your paragraphs. That means putting them into the best order.

Practise planning with others so that you share your ideas and your organisation skills. You cannot do that in an exam, but if you plan carefully with others, you will find that you plan better even when you are working on your own and have very little time.

Understanding the question

Underline the **key words** in the question, and add notes around the question. There is an example on page 63, opposite.

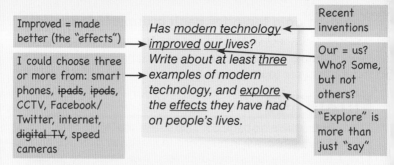

Improved = made better (the "effects")

Has modern technology improved our lives?
Write about at least three examples of modern technology, and explore the effects they have had on people's lives.

Recent inventions

Our = us? Who? Some, but not others?

I could choose three or more from: smart phones, ~~ipads~~, ~~ipods~~, CCTV, Facebook/ Twitter, internet, ~~digital TV~~, speed cameras

"Explore" is more than just "say"

Jotting down ideas

Jot down any useful thoughts you have that are likely to be relevant to the task. Don't think hard and don't worry about detail at this stage. You might jot down things like:

- Communication / staying in touch with friends
- Smart phones are everything in one place – phone, email, camera, notes, etc.
- Always being watched / no privacy.

Grouping ideas

Draw arrows or lines between ideas that might go together in natural ways.

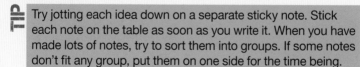

TIP

Try jotting each idea down on a separate sticky note. Stick each note on the table as soon as you write it. When you have made lots of notes, try to sort them into groups. If some notes don't fit any group, put them on one side for the time being.

Deciding on a topic for each group of ideas

Perhaps one of the ideas you have jotted down will be a useful heading (**topic heading**) for a group that it belongs to. These groups are your **topic groups**.

TRY IT OUT

Look at the table on page 65. This shows the notes one pair of students made in response to the essay question on page 62. The students have organised their ideas into groups (or columns).

Try to choose one phrase from each column that could make a rough title for the whole group column. For example, the first column could be headed *Personal communication* or just *Communication*.

If you cannot choose one phrase, then try to think of a word or short phrase that might sum up the column.

Communication			
Do we communicate before we think nowadays?	Always being watched / no privacy	If the internet or phone break down you've had it!	Can learn at own pace – find out for self
Communication / staying in touch with friends	Safety/ security – people tracked and watched	We can do things really fast ... saves time	Twitter and VLE allow us to share ideas when apart
Communication is cheap and so it is always possible	Online/ cyber bullying	You can get instant replies on Facebook. Letters so SLOW!	Internet gives access for everyone, wherever
Perhaps people used to TALK to each other more	Speed cameras are unfair	Smart phones are everything in one place – phone, email, camera, notes, etc.	Can find out everything quickly – education
Hard just to shut off and escape people	Speed cameras make cars go at slower speeds	Poor people in the world have a huge disadvantage	Can know so much nowadays!
	CCTV and speed cameras force people to behave		

Sequencing paragraphs

Four groups (or columns) of ideas would give you a six-paragraph **structure** for your writing:

Paragraph	Paragraph content
1	Answer the question directly, introducing all your topic headings. (See page 68 for an opening paragraph.)
2	Use the ideas in your first topic group for the content of this paragraph, starting with the topic heading you chose. (See column 1 in the table on page 65.)
3	Use the ideas in your second topic group for the content of this paragraph, starting with the topic heading you chose.
4	Use the ideas in your third topic group for the content of this paragraph, starting with the topic heading you chose.
5	Use the ideas in your last topic group for the content of this paragraph, starting with the topic heading you chose.
6	Try to tie it all together without repeating yourself. Are there some points that are more important than others? Are some people better off with new technology than others? This is your **conclusion**.

Structuring an opening paragraph

There are many ways to structure (or organise) an opening paragraph. Here is *one* way:

- Answer the question directly.
- Introduce the topic headings you chose as part of your essay planning.
- Do not go into detail. You will do that in the main part of the essay.

Below are the topic headings that one student chose when planning a response to the essay question on page 62:

Topic headings
1. Communication is cheap, so it is always possible / staying in touch
2. Safety/security – people tracked and watched
3. Smart phones are everything in one place – phone, email, camera, notes, etc. / convenience and power
4. Can find everything out quickly – education

Now look at the student's opening paragraph on page 68. See how the paragraph is structured around all four of the student's topic headings. He introduces some broad ideas but leaves the detail for the main paragraphs of his essay.

Here is the student's opening paragraph:

Today technology dominates our lives, but has it improved them? Much of the technology we use is fast, electronic and portable. We can carry it with us in the form of smart phones – computers in our pocket. Other technology – such as speed cameras and CCTV – follows us around. Modern technology has clearly brought many benefits: it makes communication cheap and immediate so that we can stay in touch with each other wherever we are in the world. The technology allows us to be watched over and kept safe. It is convenient – smart phones bring everything together in one pocket-sized device. Technology also gives us unlimited, instant access to knowledge and information in ways that boost our education significantly. On the other hand, the benefits might not reach everyone, and perhaps there are disadvantages for all of us.

NOTE
The student's second paragraph is based on the ideas he jotted down for his first topic heading. His third paragraph is based on the ideas under his second topic heading, and so on.

Writing good main paragraphs

One way of organising each of the main paragraphs is by using the PEE chain. Basic PEE stands for point, example, explanation (see pages 60 and 61 to recap). Your writing will be even better if you *extend* your PEE chain so that you *explore* the example and point you are making.

The student's fourth paragraph is on page 69, opposite. It is based on the third planning column from the table on page 65. Notes have been added to the first part to show you how he uses the PEE chain to organise, explain and develop his ideas.

❶ <u>Despite this</u> loss of privacy, **❷ most people find mobile technology very convenient**. Being spied on is a price they are willing to pay. **❸** <u>They love their smart phones because they keep everything in one place</u> – phone, email, camera, notes, etc. **❹ This means that the owner can always send a message, take pictures, record or look things up at a moment's notice.** **❺** <u>Of course, people who are too poor to afford smart phones have a huge disadvantage</u>: **❻** <u>by the time they find out about opportunities and events, these are no longer available.</u> **❼** <u>As a result, poorer people are greatly inconvenienced and get further behind richer people</u>. **❽ Because of that, we could say that mobile technology makes the world more and more unequal, and widens the gap between poor and rich countries.** However, becoming dependent on smart phones has a downside even for people in rich countries: if you lose or break your phone you soon discover that you cannot really do without it. When that happens you feel more miserable and stressed than if you had never had the phone in the first place. People who have never had the technology never have to suffer losing it.

❶ Links back to the previous paragraph.

❷ Point: starts with a clear point: convenience.

❸ Example: gives an example of convenience: everything in one place.

❹ Explain: introduces an explanation of why this is convenient.

❺ Point: introduces a new but relevant point about poverty and technology.

❻ Example: gives an example of how the poor lose out.

❼ Explain: the example is explained.

❽ Extend/explore: the explanation is extended and explored with a closer look at the effects of poverty.

It is by no means a perfect paragraph. You could probably improve it. Nevertheless, it is reasonably well organised, and the student has tried to use the PEE chain to stay clear and organised.

TRY IT OUT

1 Add more notes to the student's paragraph to show how he uses the PEE chain. Start from "However, becoming dependent …".

2 EITHER write your own paragraph on the third planning column OR write a paragraph on the fourth planning column (see page 65.) Then add notes to show you have used the PEE chain to organise, explain and develop your ideas.

Writing longer exam answers

Careful organisation is just as important when answering longer exam questions.

A GCSE biology exam paper explains that a student has been told to grow some bacteria on agar jelly in a Petri dish. The question says:

> Describe how the student should prepare an uncontaminated culture of the bacterium in the Petri dish.
>
> You should explain the reasons for each of the steps you describe.

On page 71, opposite, you can see how one student answered the question.

What the answer has to be about: the science knowledge

Describe how the student should prepare an *uncontaminated culture of the bacterium in the Petri dish*.

Describe/ explain = similar: need for detail, say why

"Steps" means one after the other; three steps here

You should *explain the reasons* for each of the *steps* you describe.

Here is her six-mark exam answer.

First the student should sterilise the Petri dish and agar <u>in order to</u> kill any bacteria that are not supposed to be in the experiment. Then the student should pass an inoculation loop through a flame. Next, the student must dip the sterile loop into the culture medium and spread the bacterium onto the agar. This must be done very carefully <u>as</u> the Petri dish lid must be opened only very slightly or microbes will get in and contaminate the contents of the dish. Finally, the closed dish needs to be carefully sealed with tape <u>so that</u> foreign microbes cannot get in, the culture incubates and the bacteria grow. The student must leave the dish alone for some time while the process in the dish develops. They can check the process daily through the dish, but they must not break the seal until colonies can be clearly seen, <u>because</u> that would let contamination in.

Notice how the student added notes to the question to help her keep her answer organised and clear. Her notes guide her answer.

TRY IT OUT

1   Notice how the answer uses the cause and effect connectives (underlined) to *explain why* the student should do certain things.

2   Which other category of connective are used in the answer? (See pages 25 to 27 for more about connectives.)

3   How do those connectives help?

How to make reading easier

Reading can be hard because of:

- long or unusual words
- long sentences
- ideas or information we know little about.

Here are some things you can do to make reading easier:

Problem	What you can do about it
Long or unusual words	1 Sound the word out, or break it down into parts. Do you know it now? (See pages 4 to 9 for some useful spelling strategies.)
	2 See if you can work out the meaning of the word by reading the rest of the sentence.
	3 Use a dictionary to look the word up.
Long sentences	1 Before you read the whole text, skim over it to work out what it is about. Look at headings and other clues that might tell you what the text is about. Are there any pictures or diagrams to help you?
	2 When you have done all that, you might find that hard, complicated sentences become easier to read.
Ideas or information we know little about	The advice above for long sentences will help here. If you are trying to read about new things, it is best not to get bogged down in detail straight away. Just try to concentrate on getting the gist (general meaning) of the new ideas and information.

TIP Often, reading is hard because the wrong method (or strategy) is being used. Getting good at skimming and scanning will make reading much more efficient. (See below for advice on skimming and scanning.)

Important reading strategies

Skimming: reading quickly over the surface of a text to get the gist of what it is about.

Scanning: glancing over a text until you find the information or the key words you need.

Close reading: reading a part of a text very carefully, concentrating on detail.

Below, you will find more detail on how to skim and scan effectively.

Skimming: getting the gist

When you are asked to read something, it is often a good idea to skim read it first before you read it closely and carefully. Skimming will tell you:

- roughly what the text is about
- whether it might be relevant
- whether it might be interesting.

For example, if you found a letter on the ground, you might wonder if it was interesting or important. To find out, you would skim read the letter. This would mean running your eyes over it, and picking up its gist – what it is about. Skimming the letter might tell you whether it is relevant to you. You might not go on to read every word unless your first skim suggested that reading the letter closely would be worthwhile.

When you have to read about a subject you find difficult or you know little about, skim the text first to get an overview of what it is about. If you don't like to skim read, then try reading just the first and last sentence of each paragraph.

Scanning: looking for something in a text

Scanning is another way of not reading every word, but still getting something out of a text. Here is how to scan:

1 Decide what you need to know.
2 Ask yourself which words are relevant to what you need to know. For example, if you are using a text to find out about armies in the First World War, then you could look for these key words: army, soldier, battle, uniform, troops. You could also find dates by looking for numbers.
3 Run your eyes over the text and look for the key words.

Only read closely and carefully when you think you might have found something useful.

When you are asked to read something and then answer some questions, read the questions first. Then you can look out for the question's key words as you scan the text.

TRY IT OUT

Below is a short text.

1 Skim the text to decide what it is about. Which word in the text sums up what it is about?

2 Scan the text to find out answers to these two questions:

  a How many people joined the army in the first month of recruitment?

  b Which volunteers were turned away when they tried to join the army?

> When war began, so many young men joined the army that no one had to be forced to join until 1916. For the first two years of the war, men only had to be persuaded to join the army. Popular enthusiasm meant that in the first month of recruitment about 30,000 men volunteered for the army every day. Many new recruits came from very impoverished homes and were often in poor health. In fact, although the army was desperate for all the recruits it could get, it had to reject many volunteers because their physical health was so poor.

3 Which words in the text do you find hard? Write down each hard word.

4 Read the advice about reading long or unusual words on page 73. Use the advice to work out the meaning of each hard word.

Other important reading skills

Skill	What this skill means	Some ways to practise the skill
Visualise	Form pictures in your mind of what is being written about.	• Jot down notes about (or describe to someone else) what a character in a novel looks like. • Use detail in the text to draw what a character (or a place) looks like.
Hear the writer	Imagine the voice of the writer (or narrator).	Read the text aloud, trying to use a tone of voice that expresses the attitudes and feelings of the writer.
Infer and interpret	Read between the lines.	• Think carefully about what assumptions the writer is making. • Look for clues about characters and what motivates them. • Ask yourself what a writer (or narrator) is implying (hinting).
Predict	Think about clues in the text that hint at what will happen later.	Keep asking yourself: • What is likely to happen later in the story? • What will the writer's conclusion be? • How do I know?
Re-read	Go back over parts of the text.	Re-read earlier parts of the text to remind yourself of information, events, etc.

Evaluate	Keep asking yourself how good the writing or the ideas are.	<ul><li>Think or talk about how much you agree with the writer.</li><li>Compare this text with similar ones you have read. How good is it in comparison?</li></ul>
Empathise	Put yourself 'in the shoes' of a writer or character.	<ul><li>Ask yourself what you would do (or did) in their position.</li><li>Pay attention to how a writer or a character is feeling.</li></ul>
Summarise	Briefly sum up what you have read in your own words.	When you have read something, close the book and jot down the key information you have just read. Use notes and bullet points if they help.

Reading more: the 'reading gym'

Reading is still a very important skill. One reason some people don't read well is that they don't read often enough. If you are going to get good at reading, you need to practise it a lot. The trouble is that most of us don't like practising things – especially things we don't enjoy, so here are some tips and ideas to help you practise and enjoy reading:

- Read for 15 minutes on your own at the same time every day, e.g. *7–7.15 a.m.* Do not let anything get in the way of this routine. Turn off all phones, computers, TVs, etc. Make yourself do it.

- Tell your family that you are reading every day at the same time. Ask them to do it as well. Do not give it up.

- Add one minute to your reading time on the first of every month. Do it. Do not give up.

- Read whatever you like, but try books with very few pictures. Ask friends, family, teachers and librarians to suggest books you might like.

- Watch films that have been made from good books. Talk about the film a lot. Then read the book.

- Get all your family to join the local library. All go to it. Choose books and take them out. Read them. Talk to each other about the books. Who has read them carefully? Remember: take them back in time to avoid fines.

These are ideas for exercising and building your 'reading muscles'. It's like going to the gym: many people give up, but if you stick to it, you get fitter and fitter – and in the end everyone admires you for it.

8: RESEARCH SKILLS

Reading to find things out

Sometimes you will be given the task to find something out. For example, you might be asked to find out about:

- foods that are not suitable for someone with coeliac disease
- the importance of warming down after exercise
- what theatres were like in Shakespeare's time.

Many people have no idea how to find information and ideas about subjects like these. They get into a mess, and they do a lot of pointless copying, pasting and printing.

Step-by-step research

The table below gives you the steps for how to find things out (**research**). It will help you to organise your research.

Copy out a large version of the table. Copy just the headings and text in the left-hand column. *Do not copy* any of the words in *italics* in the right-hand column. They are only there to explain the steps, or give you extra help.

Steps in the finding out process …	My notes and thoughts …
1 How shall I present what I find out? (For example, *in notes, essay, speech.*)	*You need to know how you will present the information before you start researching. There is no point spending hours on the research if at the end you have only to write five lines. An essay would mean having to do lots of work though.*

2 What do I already know about the topic I have to find out about? (See page 82 for a KWL grid.)	*It is worth jotting down what you think you already know about the topic/question. It is important for two reasons:* • *You might already know a lot.* • *It is easier to find out new things if you can add them to what you already know.*
3 What is this research for? How much detail do I need to find out?	*This will help make the research as fast as possible so that you do not get overwhelmed. Knowing how you will use what you find out will help you know how much to find out.*
4 Where should I find out? Ask someone? A book? The internet?	*Do not go straight to the internet. There might be a simpler and less distracting way of finding out what you need to know.*
5 Make brief, relevant notes when you find useful information.	*Do not copy words out (or copy and paste them). Keep thinking about the research question and what it is for, and just jot down a few notes in your own words when you find something useful. Try just to summarise information, rather than copy it.*
6 How trustworthy is the information I find?	*Do not assume that you can trust every source of information. Would you trust everything that anyone told you? Do not trust books and the internet either: they might be biased. They might be trying to sell you something, or to influence you in some way.*

WATCH OUT

It is illegal to copy other people's words into your own work. This crime is called **plagiarism**. If you want to use someone else's words, you must put quotation marks ("…") around them, and say where you found them. It is usually better to use your own words to summarise someone else's.

KWL: know / want to know / learnt

Another simple way of organising research is to use a KWL grid like the one below.

W: What I know	K: What I want to know	L: What I have learnt
If you do not warm down, then you can be left with aches and soreness.	What causes these aches and soreness?	Lactic acid and toxins build up during exercise. Warm down helps to get these out of the muscles …
You must not just stop exercise suddenly and walk away – you have got to warm down slowly.	Do some sorts of exercises need longer warm downs than other sorts?	The higher the heart rate during exercise, and the harder the muscles have worked, the longer the warm down should be …
Most gym equipment has a warm down setting or programme.	Why do people call it a <u>warm</u> down? Why isn't it always called a <u>cool</u> down? Are these different things?	

To use a KWL grid, you need to:

- Jot down what you already **k**now (**K**).
- Decide **w**hat (**W**) *more* you would like to know.
- Do the finding out, and note down what you **l**earn (**L**) that is relevant to what you wanted to know.

Look at the example on page 82. It is part of a KWL grid a student used for one of our research topics, "The importance of warming down after exercise".

TRY IT OUT

Use a KWL grid for your own research task. Copy out a much larger version of the grid. You might use a larger piece of paper, or turn it sideways (landscape), so that you have more room in each column.

Using the internet to find things out

If you just type your research question into a search engine and tap Enter, you are likely to be overwhelmed by the results. For example, Google offered over one million results for "The importance of warming down after exercise".

Consider this research question:

> *Is spinach good for us?*

Now look at the steps on pages 84 to 86. They show you how you might use the internet to help you get an answer.

1 Decide on the key words for a search	You need to decide what is meant in the question by "good" and "us". Then think of other words that might be relevant. That means you need to think about what you think you already know. Your key word list might include these words: spinach, health, vitamins, benefits, diet, nutrition.
2 Type the key words into a search engine and look at the results	The results have summaries in which your key words will appear. Skim over the summaries. Look at the words around "spinach". Which site looks most helpful and relevant? Which site uses the sort of language you will be able to cope with?
3 Choose a result and click on it	One site gave a page headed, "The Health Benefits of Spinach". It pretty much answered the question. Another site was harder to use. It was just headed, "Leafy green vegetables". It was also full of words. I could have scanned the page for my key words, but browsers have a scanning tool to make things easy. To use it, I pressed Ctrl and F. A box appeared and I typed *spinach* in it. I was immediately shown the bit of the page I needed.

4 Evaluate the website	Not all information should be trusted. For example, you might click on a site run by spinach farmers. They would not necessarily lie to you, but they might be biased. They might exaggerate the benefits of spinach. Ask yourself questions such as: • Is it in their interests to give me a particular view? • Does the information come from an expert? • Is the information up to date? (Some sites are no longer being updated.) Be very careful about information. Never rely on just one website.
5 Make notes	Do not copy text out. Just take the information you need. Summarise it *in your own words* to help you understand what you find. You could either jot down notes on paper, or write notes straight into a word processor. For the spinach question you could simply draw a line down the centre of a piece of paper. Head one side *Yes* and the other *No*, and jot down information you find on the relevant side. You could have a middle column for *Perhaps*.

6	**Rules for quotations** and making a note of where you find information	If you do copy out very short bits from web pages, then make sure you put quotation marks ("…") round the bit you have quoted.
		Make a note of where you find information (your **source**). Note down the title of the page you use and its owner. If possible, also note down the page's URL. You can copy and paste this from the top of the screen. It will look something like this:
		http://www.jimmygreens.com/nutritionandhealth-articles/leafy-green-vegetables
		Do not try to use this link though: I made it up.